Team Spirit®

THE OAKLAND RAIDERS

BY

MARK STEWART

Content Consultant
Jason Aikens

NORWOOD HOUSE PRESS

CHICAGO, ILLINOIS

Norwood House Press
P.O. Box 316598
Chicago, Illinois 60631

For information regarding Norwood House Press, please visit our website at:
www.norwoodhousepress.com or call 866-565-2900.

PHOTO CREDITS:
All photos courtesy Getty Images except the following:
Black Book Partners (6, 7, 9, 22, 35 all, 38, 39, 40 bottom, 41),
Topps, Inc. (14, 16, 20, 21, 28, 29, 30, 34 left, 36, 40 top, 43),
Associated Press (27), Matt Richman (48).
Cover photo: Paul Spinelli/Getty Images
Special thanks to Topps, Inc.

Editor: Mike Kennedy
Designer: Ron Jaffe
Project Management: Black Book Partners, LLC.
Research: Joshua Zaffos
Special thanks to Brian Ames

LIBRARY OF CONGRESS CATALOGING-IN-PUBLICATION DATA

Stewart, Mark, 1960-
  The Oakland Raiders / by Mark Stewart ; content consultant, Jason Aikens.
     p. cm. -- (Team spirit)
  Includes bibliographical references and index.
  Summary: "Presents the history and accomplishments of the Oakland
Raiders football team. Includes highlights of players, coaches, and awards,
quotes, timeline, maps, glossary, and websites"--Provided by publisher.
  ISBN-13: 978-1-59953-331-5 (library edition : alk. paper)
  ISBN-10: 1-59953-331-6 (library edition : alk. paper) 1. Oakland Raiders
(Football team)--History--Juvenile literature. I. Aikens, Jason. II. Title.

GV956.O24S74 2009
796.332'640979466--dc22

                                                         2009011910

9125

Manufactured in the United States of America.

COVER PHOTO:
The Raiders celebrate a good defensive play during a 2008 game.

Table of Contents

SPORTS WORDS & VOCABULARY WORDS: In this book, you will find many words that are new to you. You may also see familiar words used in new ways. The glossary on page 46 gives the meanings of football words, as well as "everyday" words that have special football meanings. These words appear in **bold type** throughout the book. The glossary on page 47 gives the meanings of vocabulary words that are not related to football. They appear in ***bold italic type*** throughout the book.

Meet the Raiders

Just win, baby! When you play for the Oakland Raiders, you hear those words all the time. Team owner Al Davis started the saying back in the 1960s when he bought the Raiders. Now the players hear it from their coaches, their fans, and each other. It is part of a great football *tradition*.

The Raiders are one of the most successful teams in the history of American sports. Sayings like "Pride and Poise" and "Commitment to Excellence" began in their locker room. When the Raiders take those ideas with them onto the field, the result is usually a victory. Just like their fans, they are proud to wear the team's famous "Silver and Black."

This book tells the story of the Raiders. Fans around the country think of them as "outlaws"—and they love them for it. Indeed, the Raiders hear as many cheers as they do boos when they play away from home. The players like their "bad guy" image. It has helped make the Raiders one of the most interesting—and entertaining— teams in football history.

Kirk Morrison and Nnamdi Asomugha jump for joy during a 2008 game.

Way Back When

The **American Football League (AFL)** began play in 1960. One of the league's new teams was located in Minneapolis, Minnesota. At the last moment, the owners of that club pulled out of the AFL and decided to join the **National Football League (NFL)**. The AFL placed a new team, the Raiders, in Oakland, California.

The Raiders won only nine games in their first three seasons. In 1963, Al Davis was hired to coach the team and run its business. He built the Raiders around talented, young players such as Jim Otto, Clem Daniels, Tom Flores, and Fred Williamson. Oakland had a winning record in its first season under Davis.

The Raiders kept adding good players through smart trades and the college **draft**. From 1965 to 1980, Oakland had a winning record every year. During the 1960s, the team's stars included Daryle Lamonica, Fred Biletnikoff, Billy Cannon, Warren Wells, Gene Upshaw, Ben Davidson, Tom Keating, Dan Conners, David Grayson, and Willie Brown.

In 1966, the AFL and NFL started a plan to join forces. A big step in their *strategy* was the **Super Bowl**, which matched the winner of each league for the championship of **professional** football. The Raiders won the AFL title in 1967 and played in Super Bowl II. They lost to the Green Bay Packers.

Oakland's next trip to the big game came nine years later, under head coach John Madden. Quarterback Ken Stabler led the offense. His receivers included Biletnikoff, Dave Casper, and speedy Cliff Branch. Oakland's defense was known as the "Legion of Doom." It starred John Matuszak, Otis Sistrunk, Ted Hendricks, Phil Villapiano, and Jack Tatum. This group led the Raiders to victory in Super Bowl XI.

The Raiders won the Super Bowl twice more in the early 1980s. Their coach was Flores, the club's quarterback from the 1960s. These Raiders teams were also rough and tough. Quarterback Jim Plunkett guided the offense. The team's strength was its defense, which featured Hendricks, Lester Hayes, Rod Martin, Matt Millen, and Howie Long.

The teams that won Super Bowl XV and XVIII shared the same fighting spirit. However, the first represented Oakland, while the second played in Los Angeles. In 1982, the Raiders moved to the southern part of California. They played there until 1994.

The L.A. Raiders' "homegrown" stars included Marcus Allen, Todd Christensen, Tim Brown, Bo Jackson, Steve Wisniewski, Vann McElroy, and Terry McDaniel. The team also welcomed players who had been stars with other teams. These players included Bob Golic, Jay Schroeder, Jeff Hostetler, Willie Gault, Ronnie Lott, and Mike Haynes.

The Raiders had several up-and-down seasons after returning to Oakland, but the fans still supported them. Slowly but surely the Raiders improved. They won the **West Division** of the **American Football Conference (AFC)** each season from 2000 to 2002. Quarterback Rich Gannon and defensive star Charles Woodson led this *era* of success. In January of 2003—after nearly 20 years—the Raiders returned to the Super Bowl.

LEFT: Marcus Allen glides down the field for a big gain.
ABOVE: Tim Brown, one of the top receivers in team history.

The Team Today

After winning the 2002 **AFC Championship** and playing in Super Bowl XXXVII, the Raiders were forced to rebuild again. The team had won because of its many *experienced* players. But those **veterans**—including Rich Gannon, Tim Brown, Jerry Rice, Rod Woodson, and Bill Romanowski—started to wear down. Oakland needed to replace them.

Al Davis followed his recipe for success from years past. He brought in more players with great experience, including Kerry Collins, Warren Sapp, Randy Moss, and Ray Buchanan. This time, however, the *formula* did not work. The Raiders had one poor season after another.

In recent years, the team has restocked by drafting young college stars. Players such as Justin Fargas, Michael Huff, Nnamdi Asomugha, Zach Miller, JaMarcus Russell, and Darren McFadden showed great promise. Oakland fans hope they will be the group of stars that leads the Silver and Black back to the Super Bowl.

Justin Fargas takes a handoff from JaMarcus Russell during a 2008 game.

Home Turf

Even though the Raiders belonged to Oakland, they played their first two seasons in San Francisco. During that time, they waited for a new stadium to be built in their home city. The team was still waiting in 1962, when it moved into Frank Youell Field. It was the only major sports stadium named after an *undertaker*!

Finally, in 1966, Oakland-Alameda County Stadium was ready for the Raiders. They played there until 1982, when they moved south to Los Angeles. The team stayed in L.A. for more than a *decade*. The Raiders moved back to Oakland for the 1995 season and returned to Oakland-Alameda County Stadium.

The Raiders' home has gone by a few different names over the years. Their fans just call it the "Coliseum." The Raiders share the field with the Oakland A's baseball team.

BY THE NUMBERS

- *The Raiders' stadium has 63,026 seats for football.*
- *It cost $25 million to build in the 1960s. In the 1990s, it was brought up to date at a cost of $200 million.*
- *The Raiders have not retired any uniform numbers. But Jim Otto's 00 is no longer allowed by the NFL, so it will never be worn again.*

The Raiders host the Denver Broncos for a game during the 2006 season.

Dressed for Success

The Raiders' first uniforms used the "pirate colors" of black and gold. The players wore black helmets with a white stripe and no *logo*. After Al Davis bought the team in 1963, he changed Oakland's colors to silver and black.

When Davis became the owner, he also added the team logo to the helmet. It showed a pirate wearing a football helmet, along with a shield and two crossed swords. This logo has become one of the most famous in sports.

Today, the Raiders wear black or white jerseys with silver pants.

ALAN MILLER
OAKLAND RAIDERS   FULLBACK

This is why fans call their team the "Silver and Black Attack." Normally the players wear black at home and white on the road. The Raiders wore white at home for the first time during a 2008 game when the temperature on the field soared into the 90s. The players would have been too hot wearing black.

Alan Miller models the uniform with the team's original colors.

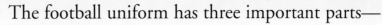

UNIFORM BASICS

The football uniform has three important parts—

- Helmet
- Jersey
- Pants

Helmets used to be made out of leather, and they did not have facemasks—ouch! Today, helmets are made of super-strong plastic. The uniform top, or jersey, is made of thick fabric. It fits snugly around a player so that tacklers cannot grab it and pull him down. The pants come down just over the knees.

There is a lot more to a football uniform than what you see on the outside. Air can be pumped inside the helmet to give it a snug, padded fit. The jersey covers shoulder pads, and sometimes a rib protector called a flak jacket. The pants include pads that protect the hips, thighs, *tailbone*, and knees.

Football teams have two sets of uniforms— one dark and one light. This makes it easier to tell two teams apart on the field. Almost all teams wear their dark uniforms at home and their light ones on the road.

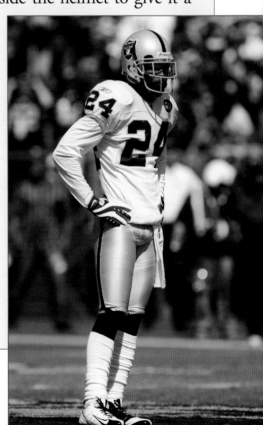

Michael Huff wears Oakland's 2008 away uniform.

We Won!

When the Raiders played in—and lost—Super Bowl II, the players thought they would get another shot at the big game soon. No one imagined it would take nine seasons. The Raiders were very good in the late 1960s and early 1970s. Oakland won its division seven times in eight seasons. But the team did not return to the Super Bowl.

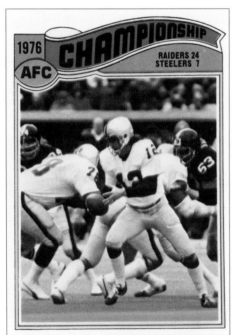

Finally, in 1976, the Raiders put it all together. They went 13–1 and won a thrilling **playoff game** against the New England Patriots. Trailing 21–10 in the fourth quarter, Ken Stabler led two late touchdown **drives** to win 24–21. In the AFC Championship, the Raiders beat the Pittsburgh Steelers.

In Super Bowl XI, Oakland felt it couldn't lose. The confident Raiders ran over the Minnesota Vikings, who were powerless to stop them. Oakland led 16–0 at halftime and 19–0 before Minnesota got on the scoreboard. Pete Banaszak then scored his second touchdown of

ABOVE: A trading card highlights Oakland's playoff victory over the Pittsburgh Steelers. **RIGHT**: Pete Banaszak rumbles over the Minnesota Vikings in Super Bowl XI.

the game. Moments later, Willie Brown returned an **interception** 75 yards for a touchdown. The final score was 32–14.

Oakland's next championship came against the Philadelphia Eagles in Super Bowl XV. The Raiders made the playoffs with a team full of *castoffs* from other clubs. Quarterback Jim Plunkett, running back Kenny King, and defensive end John Matuszak were signed by Al Davis after their old teams had given up on them.

Against the Eagles, they all played like superstars. Plunkett threw two touchdown passes in the first quarter. The first was a short pass to Cliff Branch. The

second was an 80-yard strike to King. Meanwhile, the Oakland defense was ***dominant***. Rod Martin intercepted three passes, and Matt Millen made plays all over the field. The Raiders won 27–10.

Three years later, the Raiders—now playing in Los Angeles—faced the Washington Redskins in Super Bowl XVIII. Plunkett was still the quarterback, but new young stars led the team. Marcus Allen ran for more than 1,000 yards. Tight end Todd Christensen caught more than 90 passes. The defense starred Millen, Howie Long, and Lester Hayes.

The Redskins were the defending Super Bowl champions. Earlier in the year, they had defeated the Raiders in an exciting contest, 37–35. In the first half of their rematch, star running back John Riggins could find no running room against the Raiders' defense. When the Redskins tried to pass, Hayes and Mike Haynes blanketed the Washington receivers.

The Raiders held a lead just before halftime. With 12 seconds left, Washington tried a short pass. Linebacker Jack Squirek plucked

it out of the air and ran into the end zone to make the score 21–3. Oakland poured it on in the second half. The play that broke the game wide open was a 74-yard touchdown run by Allen.

The Raiders won their third NFL Championship, 38–9. Allen set a record with 191 yards. The holder of the old record, Riggins, watched exhausted from the Washington sidelines.

LEFT: Matt Millen celebrates the Raiders' victory in Super Bowl XV.
ABOVE: Marcus Allen breaks away for his 74-yard touchdown run against the Washington Redskins.

Go-To Guys

To be a true star in the NFL, you need more than fast feet and a big body. You have to be a "go-to guy"—someone the coach wants on the field at the end of a big game. Fans of the Raiders have had a lot to cheer about over the years, including these great stars …

THE PIONEERS

JIM OTTO   Offensive Lineman

• BORN: 1/5/1938   • PLAYED FOR TEAM: 1960 TO 1974

Almost every pro team thought Jim Otto was too small when he graduated from college in 1960. He signed with the Raiders, built up his body, and played center for 15 seasons. Otto did not miss a game during his entire career in Oakland.

Fred
BILETNIKOFF
OAKLAND RAIDERS • END

FRED BILETNIKOFF   Receiver

• BORN: 2/23/1943   • PLAYED FOR TEAM: 1965 TO 1978

Too small, too slow—that is what the scouts said about Fred Biletnikoff. They left out too smart. Biletnikoff caught 40 or more passes 10 years in a row. He finished his career with 589 receptions. Biletnikoff was the last pro to play without shoulder pads.

ABOVE: Fred Biletnikoff   **RIGHT**: Art Shell

GEORGE BLANDA   Kicker/Quarterback

- BORN: 9/17/1927   • PLAYED FOR TEAM: 1967 TO 1975

George Blanda was the ultimate go-to guy for the Raiders. His clutch **field goals** helped Oakland win many games. He also was the team's backup quarterback. In 1970, Blanda passed and kicked the Raiders to the AFC title game. He retired with the pro football record of 2,002 points.

ART SHELL   Offensive Lineman

- BORN: 11/26/1946   • PLAYED FOR TEAM: 1968 TO 1982

Art Shell was big, fast, and smart. When the Oakland offense needed to open a hole, it looked to him and teammate Gene Upshaw. Later Shell became the first African-American head coach in the NFL's modern era.

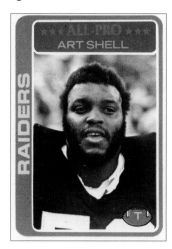

KEN STABLER   Quarterback

- BORN: 12/25/1945   • PLAYED FOR TEAM: 1968 TO 1979

Ken Stabler sat on the bench for five seasons before he got a chance to lead the Raiders. The wait was worth it. Stabler was an accurate passer who had a knack for wriggling out of tight spots. The "Snake" guided Oakland to its first Super Bowl victory.

CLIFF BRANCH   Receiver

- BORN: 8/1/1948   • PLAYED FOR TEAM: 1972 TO 1985

When the Raiders needed a first down, they threw the ball to Fred Biletnikoff or Dave Casper. When they needed a touchdown, Cliff Branch was their man. His explosive speed helped him get open for long passes. In 1976, Branch averaged more than 24 yards per catch!

LESTER HAYES   Defensive Back

- BORN: 1/22/1955
- PLAYED FOR TEAM: 1977 TO 1986

Lester Hayes was one in a long line of great Oakland pass defenders. He was extremely physical with receivers and fast enough to keep up with them as they raced down the field. Hayes helped the Raiders win two Super Bowls and was named NFL Defensive Player of the Year in 1980.

HOWIE LONG   Defensive Lineman

- BORN: 1/6/1960
- PLAYED FOR TEAM: 1981 TO 1993

Teams that played the Raiders in the 1980s usually double-teamed Howie Long. Otherwise, they were likely to lose. Long was especially good at fending off blockers. Once free, he had the speed to chase down running backs or **sack** the quarterback.

MARCUS ALLEN   Running Back

- BORN: 3/26/1960   • PLAYED FOR TEAM: 1982 TO 1992

Marcus Allen was a smooth and powerful runner. Each season from 1983 to 1985, he ran for at least 1,000 yards and caught more than 60 passes. Allen was the **Most Valuable Player (MVP)** of Super Bowl XVIII and also the NFL MVP in 1985.

TIM BROWN   Receiver

- BORN: 7/22/1966   • PLAYED FOR TEAM: 1988 TO 2003

Tim Brown spent 16 years catching passes for the Raiders—and hauled in more than 1,000 in all. He could do it all, and often did. In 1994, Brown led the AFC in pass receptions and punt returns. By the time he left the game, everyone called him "Mr. Raider."

CHARLES WOODSON   Defensive Back

- BORN: 10/7/1976   • PLAYED FOR TEAM: 1998 TO 2005

In the NFL, it can take years for a young cornerback to become a star. Charles Woodson was a standout from his very first game. In 1998, he was voted Defensive **Rookie of the Year**. Woodson was named to the **Pro Bowl** in each of his first four seasons in Oakland.

DARREN McFADDEN Running Back

- BORN: 8/27/1987
- FIRST SEASON WITH TEAM: 2008

Darren McFadden's lightning speed and sure hands made him the prize of the 2008 NFL draft. Oakland fans were thrilled that he was still available when it was the team's turn to pick. McFadden played well as a rookie and showed he could be a superstar.

LEFT: Lester Hayes
RIGHT: Darren McFadden

On the Sidelines

The Raiders have had some of the greatest coaches in the history of pro football. John Rauch, John Madden, Tom Flores, Mike Shanahan, Art Shell, Jon Gruden, Bill Callahan, and Norv Turner have all taken turns on the sidelines. Rauch, Madden, Flores, and Callahan all led the team to the Super Bowl. After Madden retired from coaching, he became a famous football broadcaster.

The man who has ruled the Raiders for more than 40 years—first as coach and then as owner—is Al Davis. He has always loved doing things his own way. In the 1960s, Davis dreamed of taking over the NFL and becoming commissioner. He built the Raiders into a winning team by finding players who were unwanted by other teams.

No team in sports has taken on the personality of its owner the way the Raiders have. Davis thinks of himself as a *renegade*. He likes players who are also proud of this reputation. Since Davis took control of the Raiders, he has had a simple *motto*: Just Win, Baby. Oakland's players, coaches, and fans feel the same way.

Coach John Madden congratulates receiver Cliff Branch during the 1976 playoffs. The Raiders won their first NFL Championship a few weeks later.

One Great Day

For many Super Bowl champs, the season comes down to one do-or-die play. After the Raiders beat the Philadelphia Eagles in Super Bowl XV, they realized how close they had come to watching the game on TV. Three weeks earlier, in Cleveland, the Raiders narrowly defeated the Browns in the second round of the playoffs.

The temperature at kickoff was 4°. It was the coldest day for an NFL game since the famous "Ice Bowl" in 1967. To make matters worse, the wind was whipping off Lake Erie. The wind chill made it feel like –37° on the field!

The Browns scored first after intercepting a pass by Jim Plunkett. The Raiders kept the score 6–0 when they crashed through the line and blocked Don Cockroft's **extra point**. It would be a long day for the Cleveland kicker.

Oakland came back a few minutes later. Plunkett handed off to Mark van Eeghen, who barreled into the end zone. The Raiders led 7–6 at halftime. Cleveland scored six points in the third quarter to regain the lead.

Mike Davis cradles the interception that sealed Oakland's playoff victory over the Cleveland Browns.

In the fourth quarter, van Eeghen finished off a long drive with a touchdown for the Raiders to make the score 14–12. Cleveland fans were frustrated. Their team should have been ahead. But Cockroft had missed two field goal tries, and his **holder** had fumbled the ball on a third attempt.

As time was running out, quarterback Brian Sipe marched the Browns down the field for one last scoring try. With the ball on the 13 yard line, Cleveland coach Sam Rutigliano called a pass play. He did not trust Cockroft to make the game-winning field goal.

Sipe faded back and saw tight end Ozzie Newsome open in the end zone. But Oakland safety Mike Davis was waiting to swoop in. As Sipe let the ball go, Davis cut in front of Newsome, made the interception, and saved the game. It was a perfect example of why the Raiders were great—they often were at their best when things were at their worst.

Legend Has It

Who was the NFL's best backup quarterback?

LEGEND HAS IT that George Blanda was. In 1970, the Raiders had two great quarterbacks: Daryle Lamonica and Ken

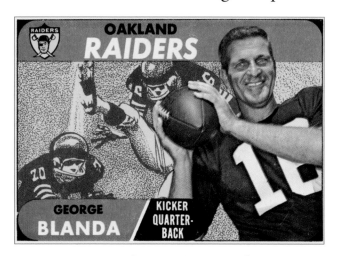

Stabler. They cut Blanda during training camp. But coach John Madden changed his mind and brought Blanda back. Starting in October, Blanda came off the bench five weeks in a row and led the Raiders to four victories and a last-second tie. Oakland won the **AFC West** by one game that season. Later in the year, the 43-year-old Blanda became the oldest player ever to suit up in a league championship game. He also won the Bert Bell Award as pro football's Player of the Year.

ABOVE: George Blanda, Oakland's amazing backup quarterback.
RIGHT: Dave Casper, the Raider known as the "Ghost."

Did a Ghost ever play for the Raiders?

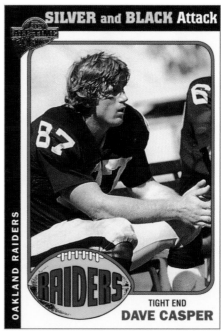

LEGEND HAS IT that one did. His name was Dave Casper. Teammates nicknamed him the "Ghost" after the cartoon character Casper the Friendly Ghost. In a 1977 playoff game against the Baltimore Colts, Casper ran a **post pattern** and caught a long pass that helped send the contest into **overtime**. To this day, Oakland fans call this famous play the "Ghost to the Post."

Who was the quietest Raider?

LEGEND HAS IT that Lester Hayes was. On a team full of big talkers, Hayes almost never said a word. That was because of a *speech impediment*. Hayes did not want opponents to make fun of him. Instead he let his great play do all his talking. Eventually, Hayes got speech therapy and corrected the problem. "Then we couldn't shut him up!" coach John Madden claims.

It Really Happened

KEN
STABLER

QUARTERBACK
RAIDERS

The Raiders are famous for their last-second victories. Most famous of all was the touchdown they scored on the final play of a game against the San Diego Chargers early in the 1978 season. Trailing 20–14 with 10 seconds left, the Raiders had the ball on San Diego's 14 yard line.

Ken Stabler dropped back to pass and scanned the field for an open teammate. In a flash, linebacker Woody Lowe crashed into Stabler near the 25 yard line. The game was over. Or was it?

Stabler **fumbled** the football, and it rolled forward. Running back Pete Banaszak picked the ball up at the 12 yard line, but he stumbled and lost control of it. Tight end Dave Casper tried to gather in Banaszak's fumble. Casper appeared to kick the ball out of his own hands. It rolled across the goal line, and he fell on it for the tying touchdown as time ran out. Errol Mann kicked the extra point to give Oakland a 21–20 win.

The Chargers were furious. They claimed that all three Raiders fumbled the ball on purpose, which was against the rules. The referees were not sure, so they did not call a penalty on Oakland. The touchdown counted—and so did the victory. Fans from both teams still argue about this play. It will forever be known as the "Holy Roller."

LEFT: Ken Stabler, the Raider who started the famous "Holy Roller" play.
ABOVE: Dave Casper catches a touchdown pass against the San Diego Chargers in 1976. Two years later, he beat them again, this time by finishing off the "Holy Roller."

Team Spirit

The Raiders like to think of themselves as a scary team. Sometimes their fans are even scarier. Game day in Oakland looks like Halloween—fans wear costumes that are unbelievable! Oakland fans call themselves Raider Nation. That is because people all over America root for the team. In many cities with an NFL team, the Raiders are the second-favorite team.

The fun in Raider Nation starts long before kickoff. Some tailgating parties begin in a backyard on Friday, and then move to the stadium parking lot on Sunday morning. The most devoted Raiders fans try to get tickets for the sections of seats behind the goal posts. Everyone calls this area the "Black Hole." Almost every fan in these seats wears black.

While fans in the Black Hole create their own entertainment, the rest of the stadium cheers for the Raiderettes. They are the team's silver-and-black dance squad. Competition to be a Raiderette is fierce. Each season the squad holds tryouts—just like the team does for its players.

The Black Hole is the place where the most loyal—and the most oddly dressed—Raiders fans gather for home games.

Timeline

In this timeline, each Super Bowl is listed under the year it was played. Remember that the Super Bowl is held early in the year and is actually part of the previous season. For example, Super Bowl XLIII was played on February 1st, 2009, but it was the championship of the 2008 NFL season.

1960
The Raiders play their first season as members of the AFL.

1974
Ray Guy is the NFL's top punter.

1963
Clem Daniels leads the AFL with 1,099 rushing yards.

1973
Marv Hubbard makes the Pro Bowl for the third year in a row.

1977
Mark van Eeghen leads the AFC with 1,273 rushing yards.

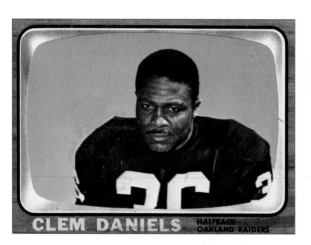

CLEM DANIELS HALFBACK OAKLAND RAIDERS

Clem Daniels

Ray Guy

Lester
Hayes

Rich
Gannon

1980
Lester Hayes is
named Defensive
Player of the Year.

1993
Kicker Jeff Jaeger
leads the NFL
in scoring.

2002
Rich Gannon is
named NFL MVP.

1984
Marcus Allen leads the
L.A. Raiders to victory
in Super Bowl XVIII.

1995
The Raiders move
back to Oakland.

2007
Nnamdi Asomugha
is named All-Pro.

Marcus
Allen

Fun Facts

IT'S A GUY THING

Punter Ray Guy had a leg like a bazooka. During the 1976 Pro Bowl, he punted a ball that hit the video screen hanging above the field in the Louisiana Superdome. Guy was voted the NFL's best all-time punter when the league picked its 75th Anniversary team in 1994.

Jim OTTO
OAKLAND RAIDERS • CENTER

OH, I GET IT

Jim Otto wore number 50 during his first year with the Raiders. The following season he got permission from the AFL to wear 00. The number—double-zero or "*aught*-oh"—was a play on Otto's name.

HONOR GUARD

After retiring from the Raiders, **All-Pro** guard Gene Upshaw became the head of the **NFL Players Association**. After he died in 2008, every player added the initials *G.U.* to their helmets in his honor.

ABOVE: Jim Otto wears his 00 jersey.
RIGHT: Clarence Davis (#28) makes his miraculous "Sea of Hands" catch.

SEA CHANGE

In 1974, the Miami Dolphins hoped to reach the Super Bowl for the fourth year in a row. The Raiders beat them 28–26 in the playoffs on a touchdown with 24 seconds left. Clarence Davis caught a desperate pass in the midst of three Dolphin defenders. The

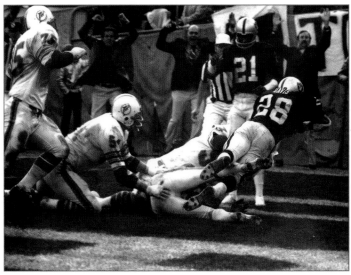

play went down in history as the "Sea of Hands."

TALL TALE

Al Davis loved tall players. In 1967, he drafted 7′ 0″ Richard Sligh and tried to make him into a defensive lineman. He also invited 6′ 7″ basketball star Rick Barry to work out with the Raiders.

SAME OLD STORY

In a 2001 game against the Kansas City Chiefs, 35-year-old Tim Brown became the oldest player ever to return a punt for a touchdown. Brown scored on an 88-yard run. It was the third time in his career that he took a punt back all the way.

Talking Football

"To be a Raider you have to be a winner. To be a winner you have to have total dedication—a burning desire to be the best."
—*Tom Flores, on what it means to be a Raider*

"In the NFL there are twenty-five guys who can throw better than I can. But I can make guys win."
—*Ken Stabler, on how he rated as a quarterback*

"Any person on the field can catch me from behind—that includes the officials."
—*Fred Biletnikoff, on his lack of speed*

"You want to play so well and be so effective that you want people to remember your name a hundred years from now."
—*Marcus Allen, on what it takes to be an all-time great*

ABOVE: Tom Flores   **RIGHT**: Steve Wisniewski

"You don't adjust. You just dominate."
—Al Davis, on the team's game plan for tough opponents

"The players on that 1976 team were very close."
—Phil Villapiano, on Oakland's first championship team

"It was an honor for me. I had great role models in Howie Long and Matt Millen."
—Steve Wisniewski, on the thrill of wearing the Silver and Black

"If King Kong and I went into an alley, only one of us would come out. And it wouldn't be the monkey."
—Lyle Alzado, on how tough he was as a player

"Everywhere I've been, I've been the screwball on the team … but here I'm just a normal guy!"
—Ted Hendricks, on joining the Raiders in 1975

For the Record

The great Raiders teams and players have left their marks on the record books. These are the "best of the best" ...

Daryle Lamonica

Marcus Allen

RAIDERS AWARD WINNERS

WINNER	AWARD	YEAR
Al Davis	AFL Coach of the Year	1963
Archie Matsos	AFL All-Star Game co-MVP	1964
Daryle Lamonica	AFL Most Valuable Player	1967
John Rauch	AFL Coach of the Year	1967
Daryle Lamonica	AFL Most Valuable Player	1969
George Blanda	AFC Most Valuable Player	1970
Ken Stabler	NFL Offensive Player of the Year	1974
Ken Stabler	NFL Most Valuable Player	1974
Fred Biletnikoff	Super Bowl XI MVP	1976
Jim Plunkett	Comeback Player of the Year	1980
Jim Plunkett	Super Bowl XV MVP	1980
Lester Hayes	NFL Defensive Player of the Year	1980
Lyle Alzado	Comeback Player of the Year	1982
Marcus Allen	NFL Offensive Rookie of the Year	1982
Marcus Allen	Super Bowl XVIII MVP	1983
Marcus Allen	NFL Offensive Player of the Year	1985
Marcus Allen	NFL Most Valuable Player	1985
Charles Woodson	NFL Defensive Rookie of the Year	1998
Rich Gannon	Pro Bowl MVP	2001
Rich Gannon	Pro Bowl MVP	2002
Rich Gannon	NFL Most Valuable Player	2002

RAIDERS ACHIEVEMENTS

ACHIEVEMENT	YEAR
AFL West Champions	1967
AFL Champions	1967
AFL West Champions	1968
AFL West Champions	1969
AFC West Champions	1970
AFC West Champions	1972
AFC West Champions	1973
AFC West Champions	1974
AFC West Champions	1975
AFC West Champions	1976
AFC Champions	1976
Super Bowl XI Champions	1976*
AFC Champions	1980
Super Bowl XV Champions	1980
AFC West Champions	1982
AFC West Champions	1983
AFC Champions	1983
Super Bowl XVIII Champions	1983
AFC West Champions	1985
AFC West Champions	1990
AFC West Champions	2000
AFC West Champions	2001
AFC West Champions	2002
AFC Champions	2002

Super Bowls are played early the following year, but the game is counted as the championship of this season.

Jim Plunkett, a leader for the 1980 and 1983 champs.

Pinpoints

T he history of a football team is made up of many smaller stories. These stories take place all over the map—not just in the city a team calls "home." Match the pushpins on these maps to the Team Facts and you will begin to see the story of the Raiders unfold!

TEAM FACTS

1 Oakland, California—*The Raiders played here starting in 1960.*

2 Los Angeles, California—*The Raiders played here from 1982 to 1994.*

3 Dallas, Texas—*Tim Brown was born here.*

4 Yazoo City, Mississippi—*Willie Brown was born here.*

5 Foley, Alabama—*Ken Stabler was born here.*

6 Chicago, Illinois—*Tom Keating was born here.*

7 Wausau, Wisconsin—*Jim Otto was born here.*

8 Welch, West Virginia—*Rod Martin was born here.*

9 Youngwood, Pennsylvania—*George Blanda was born here.*

10 Salamanca, New York—*Marv Hubbard was born here.*

11 Long Branch, New Jersey—*Phil Villapiano was born here.*

12 Barcelona, Spain—*The Raiders won the* **American Bowl** *here in 1994.*

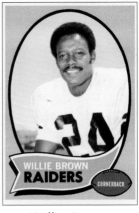

Willie Brown

Play Ball

Football is a sport played by two teams on a field that is 100 yards long. The game is divided into four 15-minute quarters. Each team must have 11 players on the field at all times. The group that has the ball is called the offense. The group trying to keep the offense from moving the ball forward is called the defense.

A football game is made up of a series of "plays." Each play starts and ends with a referee's signal. A play begins when the center snaps the ball between his legs to the quarterback. The quarterback then gives the ball to a teammate, throws (or "passes") the ball to a teammate, or runs with the ball himself. The job of the defense is to tackle the player with the ball or stop the quarterback's pass. A play ends when the ball (or player holding the ball) is "down." The offense must move the ball forward at least 10 yards every four downs. If it fails to do so, the other team is given the ball. If the offense has not made 10 yards after three downs—and does not want to risk losing the ball—it can kick (or "punt") the ball to make the other team start from its own end of the field.

At each end of a football field is a goal line, which divides the field from the end zone. A team must run or pass the ball over the goal line to score a touchdown, which counts for six points. After scoring a touchdown, a team can try a short kick for one "extra point," or try again to run or pass across the goal line for two points. Teams can score three points from anywhere on the field by kicking the ball between the goal posts. This is called a field goal.

The defense can score two points if it tackles a player while he is in his own end zone. This is called a safety. The defense can also score points by taking the ball away from the offense and crossing the opposite goal line for a touchdown. The team with the most points after 60 minutes is the winner.

Football may seem like a very hard game to understand, but the more you play and watch football, the more "little things" you are likely to notice. The next time you are at a game, look for these plays:

PLAY LIST

BLITZ—A play in which the defense sends extra tacklers after the quarterback. If the quarterback sees a blitz coming, he passes the ball quickly. If he does not, he can end up at the bottom of a very big pile!

DRAW—A play in which the offense pretends it will pass the ball, and then gives it to a running back. If the offense can "draw" the defense to the quarterback and his receivers, the running back should have lots of room to run.

FLY PATTERN—A play in which a team's fastest receiver is told to "fly" past the defensive backs for a long pass. Many long touchdowns are scored on this play.

SQUIB KICK—A play in which the ball is kicked a short distance on purpose. A squib kick is used when the team kicking off does not want the other team's fastest player to catch the ball and run with it.

SWEEP—A play in which the ball carrier follows a group of teammates moving sideways to "sweep" the defense out of the way. A good sweep gives the runner a chance to gain a lot of yards before he is tackled or forced out of bounds.

Glossary

AFC CHAMPIONSHIP—The game played to determine which American Football Conference (AFC) team will go to the Super Bowl.

AFC WEST—A division for teams that play in the western part of the country.

ALL-PRO—An honor given to the best players at their position at the end of each season.

AMERICAN BOWL—An NFL preseason game played outside of the United States.

AMERICAN FOOTBALL CONFERENCE (AFC)—One of two groups of teams that make up the NFL. The winner of the AFC plays the winner of the National Football Conference (NFC) in the Super Bowl.

AMERICAN FOOTBALL LEAGUE (AFL)—The football league that began play in 1960 and later merged with the NFL.

DRAFT—The annual meeting during which teams choose from a group of the best college players. The draft is held each spring.

DRIVES—Series of plays by the offense that "drive" the defense back toward its own goal line.

EXTRA POINT—A kick worth one point, attempted after a touchdown.

FIELD GOALS—Goals from the field, kicked over the crossbar and between the goal posts. A field goal is worth three points.

FUMBLED—Lost control of the ball.

HOLDER—The player who keeps the ball steady for the kicker.

INTERCEPTION—A pass that is caught by the defensive team.

MOST VALUABLE PLAYER (MVP)—The award given each year to the league's best player; also given to the best player in the Super Bowl and Pro Bowl.

NATIONAL FOOTBALL LEAGUE (NFL)—The league that started in 1920 and is still operating today.

NFL PLAYERS ASSOCIATION—The organization that represents the NFL players in all business matters.

OVERTIME—The extra period played when a game is tied after 60 minutes.

PLAYOFF GAME—A game played after the season to determine which teams play for the championship.

POST PATTERN—A play that calls for a receiver to run toward the goal post.

PRO BOWL—The NFL's all-star game, played after the Super Bowl.

PROFESSIONAL—A player or team that plays a sport for money.

ROOKIE OF THE YEAR—The annual award given to the league's best first-year player.

SACK—Tackle of the quarterback behind the line of scrimmage.

SUPER BOWL—The championship of football, played between the winners of the NFC and AFC. In the 1960s, the winners of the AFL and NFL played each other in the Super Bowl.

VETERANS—Players with great experience.

WEST DIVISION—A group of teams that play in the western part of the country.

OTHER WORDS TO KNOW

AUGHT—Another term for zero.

CASTOFFS—People who are considered useless or are unwanted.

DECADE—A period of 10 years; also specific periods, such as the 1950s.

DOMINANT—Ruling or controlling.

ERA—A period of time in history.

EXPERIENCED—Having knowledge and skill in a job.

FORMULA—A plan or method for how to achieve a goal.

LOGO—A symbol or design that represents a company or team.

MOTTO—A short expression used again and again.

RENEGADE—Someone who rejects the normal way of doing things.

SPEECH IMPEDIMENT—A condition that prevents a person from speaking normally.

STRATEGY—A plan or method for succeeding.

TAILBONE—The bone that protects the base of the spine.

TRADITION—A belief or custom that is handed down from generation to generation.

UNDERTAKER—A person whose business is preparing the dead for burial.

Places to Go

ON THE ROAD

OAKLAND RAIDERS
7000 Coliseum Way
Oakland, California 94621
(510) 864-5000

THE PRO FOOTBALL HALL OF FAME
2121 George Halas Drive NW
Canton, Ohio 44708
(330) 456-8207

ON THE WEB

THE NATIONAL FOOTBALL LEAGUE   www.nfl.com
* *Learn more about the National Football League*

THE OAKLAND RAIDERS   www.raiders.com
* *Learn more about the Oakland Raiders*

THE PRO FOOTBALL HALL OF FAME   www.profootballhof.com
* *Learn more about football's greatest players*

ON THE BOOKSHELF

To learn more about the sport of football, look for these books at your library or bookstore:

* Stewart, Mark and Kennedy, Mike. *Touchdown: the Power and Precision of Football's Perfect Play*. Minneapolis, Minnesota: Millbrook Press, 2009.
* Buckley Jr., James. *The Child's World Encyclopedia of the NFL*. Mankato, Minnesota: Child's World, 2008.
* Gigliotti, Jim. *Football*. Ann Arbor, Michigan: Cherry Lake Publishing, 2009.
* Jacobs, Greg. *The Everything Kids' Football Book: the all-time greats, legendary teams, today's superstars—and tips on playing like a pro*. Cincinnati, Ohio: Adams Media, 2008.

Index

PAGE NUMBERS IN **BOLD** REFER TO ILLUSTRATIONS.

The Team

MARK STEWART has written more than 50 books on football, and over 200 sports books for kids. He grew up in New York City during the 1960s rooting for the Giants and Jets, and now takes his two daughters, Mariah and Rachel, to watch them play in their home state of New Jersey. Mark comes from a family of writers. His grandfather was Sunday Editor of *The New York Times* and his mother was Articles Editor of *The Ladies' Home Journal* and *McCall's*. Mark has profiled hundreds of athletes over the last 20 years. He has also written several books about New York and New Jersey. Mark is a graduate of Duke University, with a degree in History. He lives with his daughters and wife Sarah overlooking Sandy Hook, New Jersey.

JASON AIKENS is the Collections Curator at the Pro Football Hall of Fame. He is responsible for the preservation of the Pro Football Hall of Fame's collection of artifacts and memorabilia and obtaining new donations of memorabilia from current players and NFL teams. Jason has a Bachelor of Arts in History from Michigan State University and a Master's in History from Western Michigan University where he concentrated on sports history. Jason has been working for the Pro Football Hall of Fame since 1997; before that he was an intern at the College Football Hall of Fame. Jason's family has roots in California and has been following the St. Louis Rams since their days in Los Angeles, California. He lives with his wife Cynthia and their daughter Angelina in Canton, Ohio.